LUNCHBOX

DEVOTIONS FOR KIDS

May God's
Word bless you.
Myrna Conrad

MYRNA CONRAD

ISBN 978-1-68517-791-1 (paperback)
ISBN 978-1-68517-792-8 (digital)

Christian Faith Publishing
832 Park Avenue
Meadville, PA 16335
www.christianfaithpublishing.com

Printed in the United States of America

INTRODUCTION

When my son was in school, he did not like the lunches available for purchase at school and decided to start taking his lunch to school each day. I bought some paper bags and started packing a lunch for him each morning.

One morning I decided I would share a verse of scripture from my morning devotion and a thought for the day about that verse. All day I wondered what he would think of my little note in his lunch. When he got home from school, he didn't say anything about it. After several days, I decided maybe I shouldn't do that anymore. Maybe it was not something he was even reading. When he came home from school that day, he asked, "Where was my verse today? I really missed that." Well, as a mother, that warmed my heart, and I determined to continue my little notes for as long as he took his lunch to school, which happened to be until he graduated.

My husband, Bob, and I went to an awards presentation his senior year, and there was a reception afterward. To my amazement, several teachers and students came up and told me that the daily verses I put in my son's lunches had meant so much to them throughout the year. My daughter is three years older, and I wish I had thought of the idea before she graduated.

There are so many things that go on in our children's lives during their days at school. It is encouraging for them to know that their parent(s) are thinking about them and to have a note of encouragement in with their lunch. Spiritual food is just as important for their minds as physical food is for their bodies. Reinforcing God's love for your children each day will ultimately draw them closer to Him and influence how they react with those around them.

The purpose of this book is to give you the opportunity to find an appropriate verse and thought within the book and then add your personal note of encouragement to your child. The scriptures are short but powerful. It should be appropriate for any age as long as they know how to read. The pages are meant to be removed and placed in your child's lunchbox or bag. The pages are not dated because your child may be struggling with something at school and you can then find an appropriate message for that situation. My hope is that this book of short scriptures and thoughts will encourage your child(ren) as they did mine.

I have noted the translation of the Bible used for each scripture.

The illustrations are done by Marcie Caddell, four of which are representative of my grandchildren, Bryce, Sydney, Hank, and Joshua.

Don't praise yourself. Let someone
else do it. (Proverbs 27:2 ICB)

When you are tempted to brag, remember
that you don't need to. God sees you and
loves you! Just keep being you, and others
will see His light shining through you.

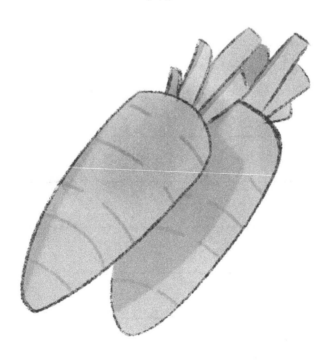

PARENT'S COMMENTS

_____

_____

_____

_____

_____

_____

_____

_____

_____

_____

_____

This is my command—be strong and courageous! Do not be afraid or discouraged. For the Lord your God is with you wherever you go. (Joshua 1:9 NLT)

Be strong and brave today in whatever you do. God is with you!

PARENT'S COMMENTS

_____

_____

_____

_____

_____

_____

_____

_____

_____

_____

_____

Honor your father and your mother, so that you may live long in the land the Lord your God is giving you. (Exodus 20:12 NIV)

It is important to obey your parents. This pleases God.

PARENT'S COMMENTS

_____

_____

_____

_____

_____

_____

_____

_____

_____

_____

_____

_____

Believe in the Lord Jesus, and you will be saved. (Acts 16:31b ICB)

Jesus wants you to believe in Him and trust Him. He loves you very much.

PARENT'S COMMENTS

_____

_____

_____

_____

_____

_____

_____

_____

_____

_____

_____

The Lord is good to everyone. He showers compassion on all his creation. (Psalm 145:9 NLT)

God is good to all and takes care of us all. Be kind to those around you today.

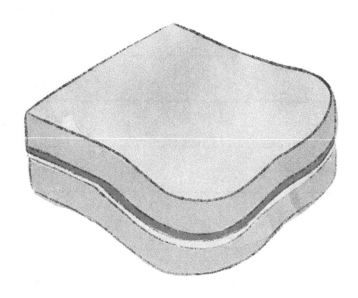

PARENT'S COMMENTS

_____

_____

_____

_____

_____

_____

_____

_____

_____

_____

_____

You are God who sees me.
(Genesis 16:13b ICB)

God sees all that is happening in
your day. If you are having a great
day, thank Him. If you are having
a hard day, ask Him for help.

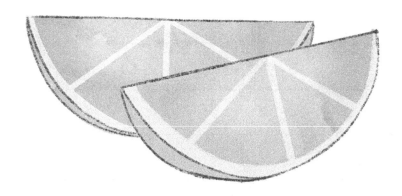

PARENT'S COMMENTS

_____

_____

_____

_____

_____

_____

_____

_____

_____

_____

_____

_____

Rejoice in the Lord always. I will say it again: Rejoice! (Philippians 4:4 NIV)

It's not always easy to be happy
all the time but you can always
be glad you are loved by God.

PARENT'S COMMENTS

_____

_____

_____

_____

_____

_____

_____

_____

_____

_____

_____

A truthful witness does not
lie. (Proverbs 14:5a ICB)

Be careful to tell the truth
about everything today.

PARENT'S COMMENTS

_____

_____

_____

_____

_____

_____

_____

_____

_____

_____

_____

_____

The Lord bless you and keep you. (Numbers 6:24 NIV)

Look for God's blessings today, and let's share them when you get home.

PARENT'S COMMENTS

_____

_____

_____

_____

_____

_____

_____

_____

_____

_____

_____

_____

Do all these things, but most important love each other. Love is what holds you all together in perfect unity. (Colossians 3:14 ICB)

If you show love to those around you, everyone will get along better.

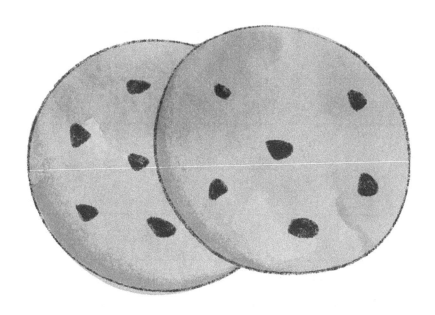

PARENT'S COMMENTS

_____

_____

_____

_____

_____

_____

_____

_____

_____

_____

_____

Let the message about Christ,
in all its richness, fill your lives.
(Colossians 3:16a NLT)

Remember to think about God's Word today. It will help you in all that you do.

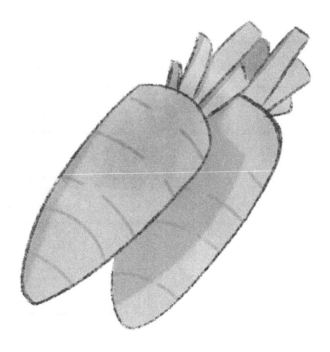

PARENT'S COMMENTS

_____

_____

_____

_____

_____

_____

_____

_____

_____

_____

_____

_____

Loving God means obeying his commands, and God's commands are not too hard for us. (1 John 5:3 ICB)

Think about what you are about to do and make sure it will be pleasing to God.

PARENT'S COMMENTS

_____

_____

_____

_____

_____

_____

_____

_____

_____

_____

_____

_____

Keep on loving each other as brothers in Christ. (Hebrews 13:1 ICB)

Brotherly love doesn't just mean loving your brother or sister; it means loving all those people around you.

PARENT'S COMMENTS

_____

_____

_____

_____

_____

_____

_____

_____

_____

_____

_____

Let everything that has breath praise the Lord! Praise the Lord! (Psalm 150:6 ESV)

Are you breathing today? Then tell God how awesome He is.

PARENT'S COMMENTS

_____

_____

_____

_____

_____

_____

_____

_____

_____

_____

_____

_____

Be very careful about what you think. Your thoughts run your life. (Proverbs 4:23 ICB)

If you think about good things, you will do good things. So try to think only good thoughts today.

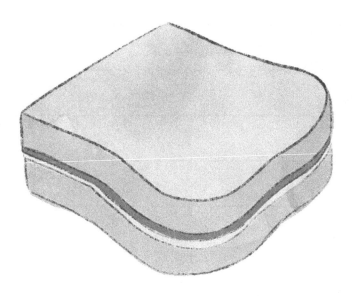

PARENT'S COMMENTS

_____

_____

_____

_____

_____

_____

_____

_____

_____

_____

_____

_____

For everyone has sinned; we all fall short of God's glorious standard. (Romans 3:23 NLT)

We all do things wrong, but God is always waiting to forgive us. We just have to ask.

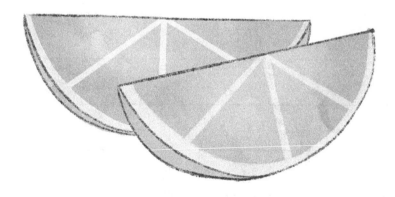

PARENT'S COMMENTS

_____

_____

_____

_____

_____

_____

_____

_____

_____

_____

_____

Everyone who calls on the
name of the Lord will be saved.
(Romans 10:13 NIV)

God loves you and wants you
to talk to Him. He wants you to
follow Him your whole life.

PARENT'S COMMENTS

_____

_____

_____

_____

_____

_____

_____

_____

_____

_____

_____

_____

You are the light of the world.
(Matthew 5:14a NLT)

Let your light shine brightly today.

PARENT'S COMMENTS

_____

_____

_____

_____

_____

_____

_____

_____

_____

_____

_____

The Lord is kind and shows mercy.
He does not become angry quickly
but is full of love. (Psalm 145:8 ICB)

God is kind and loving, so why
don't you try to be kind to everyone
around you today too.

PARENT'S COMMENTS

_____

_____

_____

_____

_____

_____

_____

_____

_____

_____

_____

Children always obey your
parents, for this pleases the
Lord. (Colossians 3:20 NLT)

It is important to obey those God has put
in charge of you because that honors God.

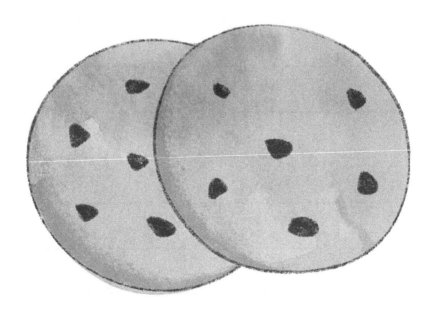

PARENT'S COMMENTS

_____

_____

_____

_____

_____

_____

_____

_____

_____

_____

_____

_____

Let your patience show itself perfectly in what you do. (James 1:4a ICB)

Patience means waiting until the right time. Be patient whenever you have to wait your turn today.

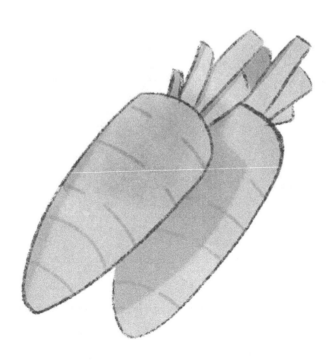

PARENT'S COMMENTS

_____

_____

_____

_____

_____

_____

_____

_____

_____

_____

_____

It is enough for students to be like their teachers… (Matthew 10:25a NIV)

Jesus is your most important teacher.
Try to love others like He does.

PARENT'S COMMENTS

_____

_____

_____

_____

_____

_____

_____

_____

_____

_____

_____

_____

When you are angry, do not sin.
And do not go on being angry
all day. (Ephesians 4:26 ICB)

Everyone gets angry at times, but God
doesn't want you to stay angry. Ask Him
to help you not be angry, and He will.

PARENT'S COMMENTS

_____

_____

_____

_____

_____

_____

_____

_____

_____

_____

_____

_____

This is what God commands: that we believe in his Son, Jesus Christ and that we love each other, just as he commanded. (1 John 3:23 ICB)

Some people are hard to love. The best way to love someone you don't feel love toward is to do an act of kindness for them.

PARENT'S COMMENTS

_____

_____

_____

_____

_____

_____

_____

_____

_____

_____

_____

When I am afraid, I will put my trust in you. (Psalm 56:3 NLT)

There are many things that make us afraid. If you are facing one of those today, trust God to take care of you.

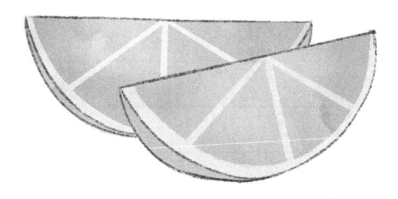

PARENT'S COMMENTS

_____

_____

_____

_____

_____

_____

_____

_____

_____

_____

_____

_____

This is the day the Lord has made. Let us rejoice and be glad today! (Psalm 118:24 ICB)

God, who is always faithful, made this day and put you just where you are to live in it. That is reason to celebrate and be happy today.

PARENT'S COMMENTS

_____

_____

_____

_____

_____

_____

_____

_____

_____

_____

_____

_____

With all my heart I try to obey you, God. Do not let me break your commands. (Psalm 119:10 ICB)

God wants us to obey Him because it is the best thing for us. Everyday pray that He will help you obey Him.

PARENT'S COMMENTS

Give thanks to the Lord for he is good. His faithful love endures forever. (Psalm 136:1 NLT)

God's love for you never changes and never stops. No matter what happens in your day today, know that He loves you.

PARENT'S COMMENTS

_____

_____

_____

_____

_____

_____

_____

_____

_____

_____

_____

Do for other people what you want them to do for you. (Luke 6:31 ICB)

If you want someone to be nicer to you, try being nicer to them.

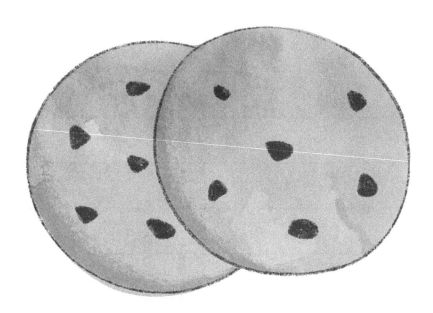

PARENT'S COMMENTS

_____

_____

_____

_____

_____

_____

_____

_____

_____

_____

_____

_____

For I can do everything through
Christ, who gives me strength.
(Philippians 4:13 NLT)

*If you are facing something you
think you can't do today, know that
with Jesus's help, you can do it!*

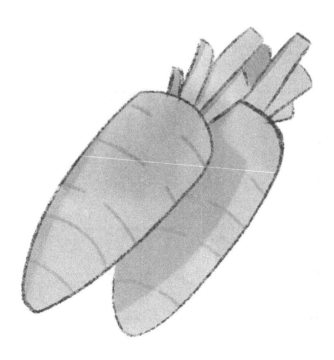

PARENT'S COMMENTS

_____

_____

_____

_____

_____

_____

_____

_____

_____

_____

_____

_____

I give you thanks, O Lord, with all my heart... (Psalm 138:1a NLT)

Think of something good that has happened to you, and thank God for that with your whole heart.

PARENT'S COMMENTS

_____

_____

_____

_____

_____

_____

_____

_____

_____

_____

_____

I am the good shepherd. The good
shepherd lays down his life for
the sheep. (John 10:11 ESV)

Jesus tells us He is the Shepherd and
we are His sheep. He is a very good
Shepherd and will always take care of us.

PARENT'S COMMENTS

_____

_____

_____

_____

_____

_____

_____

_____

_____

_____

_____

_____

Every word of God can be
trusted. (Proverbs 30:5a ICB)

Sometimes it is hard to know what is
true and what is false. The best place
to look for truth is in God's Word.

PARENT'S COMMENTS

_____

_____

_____

_____

_____

_____

_____

_____

_____

_____

_____

_____

No one can serve two masters.
(Matthew 6:24a ESV)

Whatever you put first in your life is your master. God wants to be first in your life. You can't have two firsts, so choose Him.

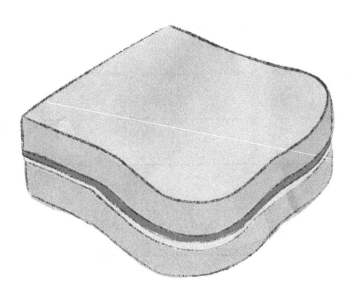

PARENT'S COMMENTS

_____

_____

_____

_____

_____

_____

_____

_____

_____

_____

_____

Love God with all your heart, soul and strength. (Deuteronomy 6:5 ICB)

God loves you and takes care of you every day. Love Him back more than you love anyone else.

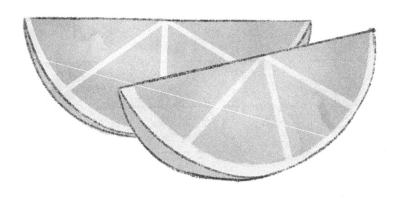

PARENT'S COMMENTS

_____

_____

_____

_____

_____

_____

_____

_____

_____

_____

_____

_____

Love your neighbor as yourself.
(Matthew 22:39b NIV)

Your neighbor is anyone that God has you around today. God wants us to love and take care of ourselves, but He also wants us to love those around us.

PARENT'S COMMENTS

_____

_____

_____

_____

_____

_____

_____

_____

_____

_____

_____

_____

So if you eat, or if you drink, or if you do anything, do everything for the glory of God. (1 Corinthians 10:31 ICB)

Have you ever done something so someone would notice you or be proud of you? Today, do the things you do to make God proud of you.

PARENT'S COMMENTS

_____

_____

_____

_____

_____

_____

_____

_____

_____

_____

_____

Some trust in chariots and some in horses, but we trust in the name of the Lord our God. (Psalm 20:7 NIV)

In the Bible, the army that had chariots and horses usually won. However, God tells us not to trust anything to help us win but Him.

PARENT'S COMMENTS

_____

_____

_____

_____

_____

_____

_____

_____

_____

_____

_____

In the beginning God created
the heavens and the earth.
(Genesis 1:1 NIV)

God created everything that
exists or has ever existed. Don't
let anyone tell you otherwise.

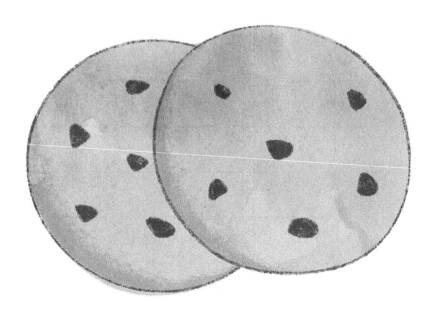

PARENT'S COMMENTS

_____

_____

_____

_____

_____

_____

_____

_____

_____

_____

_____

_____

Lord, you do everything for me. Lord, your love continues forever. You made us. Do not leave us. (Psalm 138:8 ICB)

God loves you very much, and He will take care of everything you need. He has promised never to leave you.

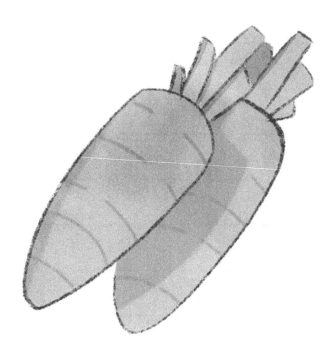

PARENT'S COMMENTS

_____

_____

_____

_____

_____

_____

_____

_____

_____

_____

_____

Do not be afraid, for I am with you. (Isaiah 43:5a NIV)

We don't have to ever be afraid, because God has promised to always be with us.

PARENT'S COMMENTS

_____

_____

_____

_____

_____

_____

_____

_____

_____

_____

_____

We must obey God rather than any human authority. (Acts 5:29b NLT)

If someone is trying to get you to do something, make sure it is something that God would want you to do before you do it.

PARENT'S COMMENTS

_____

_____

_____

_____

_____

_____

_____

_____

_____

_____

_____

Never stop praying.
(1 Thessalonians 5:17 NLT)

You can silently pray to God at any time. He wants you to talk to Him all throughout your day.

PARENT'S COMMENTS

_____

_____

_____

_____

_____

_____

_____

_____

_____

_____

_____

We love because God first
loved us. (1 John 4:19 ICB)

*If you are finding it hard to love
someone, think about how much God
loves you, and then it will be easier.*

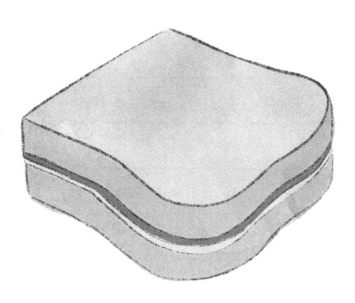

PARENT'S COMMENTS

_____

_____

_____

_____

_____

_____

_____

_____

_____

_____

_____

Be still, and know that I am
God! (Psalm 46:10a NLT)

We are always so busy, and there is so much noise in our world. You need to take moments in your day to be quiet and still, knowing that God is right there with you.

PARENT'S COMMENTS

_____

_____

_____

_____

_____

_____

_____

_____

_____

_____

_____

_____

Only the Lord gives wisdom. Knowledge and understanding come from him. (Proverbs 2:6 ICB)

Wisdom means knowing the right thing to do. God will always show you the right way.

PARENT'S COMMENTS

_____

_____

_____

_____

_____

_____

_____

_____

_____

_____

_____

The path of life of the people
who are right with God is
level. (Isaiah 26:7 ICB)

Have you ever walked on a bumpy
path or sidewalk? It is hard to walk
straight. When you do the things that
are good and right, it is like walking on
a smooth path. The way is always easier.

PARENT'S COMMENTS

_____

_____

_____

_____

_____

_____

_____

_____

_____

_____

_____

Jesus wept. (John 11:35 ESV)

Did you know that Jesus was sad sometimes, just like we are? We can always turn to Him with our feelings, and He will understand.

PARENT'S COMMENTS

_____

_____

_____

_____

_____

_____

_____

_____

_____

_____

_____

_____

Children are a gift from the
Lord. (Psalm 127:3a ICB)

You are a gift from God, and you
are so special to Him and to me.
I am very thankful for you.

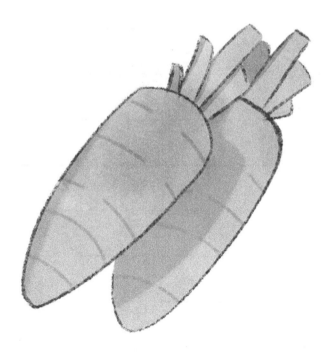

PARENT'S COMMENTS

_____

_____

_____

_____

_____

_____

_____

_____

_____

_____

_____

_____

Remember the Lord in everything you do. And he will give you success. (Proverbs 3:6 ICB)

If you ask God to help you in everything you do, He will. Then the things you do will turn out good.

PARENT'S COMMENTS

_____

_____

_____

_____

_____

_____

_____

_____

_____

_____

_____

The thing you should want most
is God's kingdom and doing what
God wants. Then all these other
things you need will be given
to you. (Mathew 6:33 ICB)

*God wants you to focus on Him first and
trust Him to give you everything you need.*

PARENT'S COMMENTS

_____

_____

_____

_____

_____

_____

_____

_____

_____

_____

_____

Be kind and compassionate to
one another, forgiving each other,
just as in Christ God forgave
you. (Ephesians 4:32 NIV)

Be kind to someone around you today,
even if they are not kind to you.

PARENT'S COMMENTS

It always gives me the greatest
joy when I hear that my
children are following the way
of truth. (3 John 1:4 ICB)

Truth is found in your Bible. God tells us
how He wants us to live, and it makes Him
very happy when we follow Him and obey.

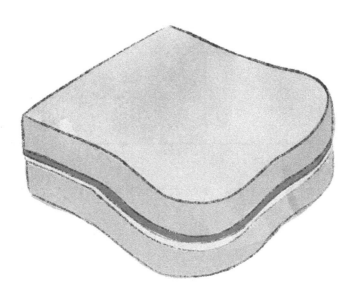

PARENT'S COMMENTS

_____

_____

_____

_____

_____

_____

_____

_____

_____

_____

_____

_____

Do what God's teaching says; do not just listen and do nothing. (James 1:22a ICB)

God doesn't just want us to listen to His Word. He wants us to do what it says.

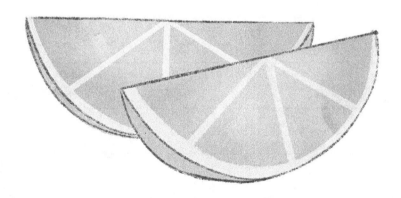

PARENT'S COMMENTS

_____

_____

_____

_____

_____

_____

_____

_____

_____

_____

You made me and formed
me with your hands. Give me
understanding so I can learn your
commands. (Psalm 119:73 ICB)

God made us, and He knows exactly
what we need. Therefore, we need
to listen to Him and obey.

PARENT'S COMMENTS

_____

_____

_____

_____

_____

_____

_____

_____

_____

_____

_____

_____

Whoever accepts a little child in my name accepts me. (Matthew 18:5 ICB)

God places such great value on you that He tells us that when anyone is nice to you, it is like they are being nice to Him.

PARENT'S COMMENTS

_____

_____

_____

_____

_____

_____

_____

_____

_____

_____

Come, my children, listen to
me; I will teach you the fear of
the Lord. (Psalm 34:11 NIV)

To fear God doesn't mean to be afraid of
Him. It means to show Him respect and to
understand that He is very powerful and
wants you to love Him and listen to Him.

PARENT'S COMMENTS

_____

_____

_____

_____

_____

_____

_____

_____

_____

_____

Even a child is known by his behavior.
His actions show if he is innocent
and good. (Proverbs 20:11 ICB)

People will know who you are by the
way you act. Be kind to others today.

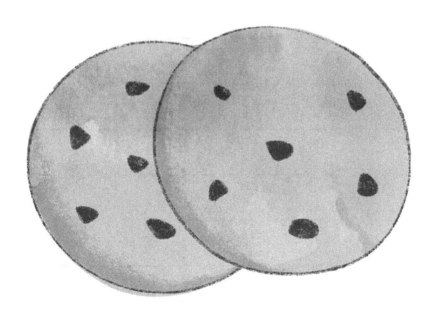

PARENT'S COMMENTS

_____

_____

_____

_____

_____

_____

_____

_____

_____

_____

_____

"You are young, but do not let anyone treat you as if you were not important." (1 Timothy 4:12a ICB)

You may be young, but you are important. People watch you, and you can make a difference in their lives by the way you live yours.

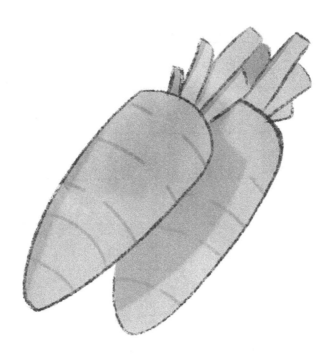

PARENT'S COMMENTS

_____

_____

_____

_____

_____

_____

_____

_____

_____

_____

_____

_____

In the same way, younger men (people) should be willing to be under older men (people). (1 Peter 5:5a ICB)

You have teachers who are in charge of what you do each day. Unless they are trying to get you to do something that you know is wrong, listen to them and show them respect.

PARENT'S COMMENTS

_____

_____

_____

_____

_____

_____

_____

_____

_____

_____

_____

They replied, "Believe in the Lord Jesus, and you will be saved." (Acts 16:31a NLT)

If you listen to Jesus, you will be saved from so many things that could harm you.

PARENT'S COMMENTS

_____

_____

_____

_____

_____

_____

_____

_____

_____

_____

_____

Think about the things of
heaven, not the things of earth.
(Colossians 3:2 NLT)

What do you think heaven will be like?
It is wonderful to imagine what it will
be like to be healthy and happy all the
time and to spend every day with Jesus.

PARENT'S COMMENTS

_____

_____

_____

_____

_____

_____

_____

_____

_____

_____

_____

Worry makes a person feel as
if he is carrying a heavy load.
But a kind word cheers up a
person. (Proverbs 12:25 ICB)

If you see someone who looks upset
or worried today, say a kind word
to them, and cheer them up.

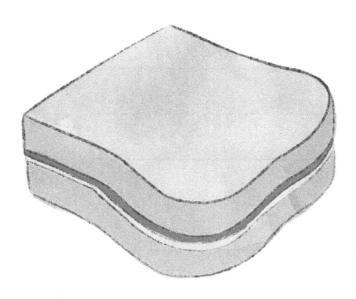

PARENT'S COMMENTS

_____

_____

_____

_____

_____

_____

_____

_____

_____

_____

_____

God is against the proud, but he gives grace to the humble. (James 4: 6b ICB)

God doesn't like it when people think they know everything. God knows more than anyone else. He always knows what is best for you. He wants you to realize that and listen to Him and obey.

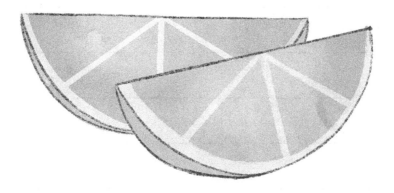

PARENT'S COMMENTS

_____

_____

_____

_____

_____

_____

_____

_____

_____

_____

_____

But some people did accept him. They believed in him. To them he gave the right to become children of God. (John 1:12 ICB)

Do you know that if you believe in Jesus, you are God's child? God is King over all, so that makes you a child of the King.

PARENT'S COMMENTS

Respect for the Lord will teach
you wisdom. If you want to
be honored, you must not be
proud. (Proverbs 15:33 ICB)

Respect and love God, and know that
He is greater than anyone else. He
wants us to understand this because it
will make us choose the right thing.

PARENT'S COMMENTS

A person may think up plans.
But the Lord decides what he
will do. (Proverbs 16:9 ICB)

When you woke up this morning, you may
have thought you knew exactly how your
day would go. However, things may have
changed. Don't worry, God is in-charge of
your whole day, and He will make it good.

PARENT'S COMMENTS

_____

_____

_____

_____

_____

_____

_____

_____

_____

_____

_____

_____

There is a right time for everything. Everything on earth has its special season. (Ecclesiastes 3:1 ICB)

Which season do you like best: summer, spring, fall, or winter? Every season has beauty in it. In the same way, there will be good days and hard days, but there is good in every day. Every day has a purpose.

PARENT'S COMMENTS

_____

_____

_____

_____

_____

_____

_____

_____

_____

_____

_____

Yet God has made everything
beautiful for its own time.
(Ecclesiastes 3:11a NLT)

You are beautiful, and God is making
you more beautiful every day.

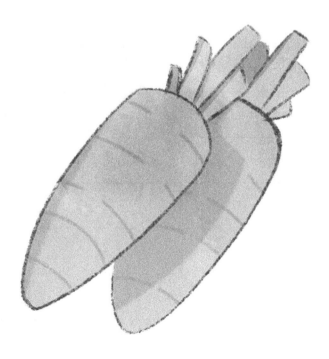

PARENT'S COMMENTS

_____

_____

_____

_____

_____

_____

_____

_____

_____

_____

_____

_____

So let's not get tired of doing what is good. (Galatians 6:9a NLT)

Sometimes it is very hard and very tiring to try to be good every day. God tells us to keep trying, and He also tells us He will help us.

PARENT'S COMMENTS

_____

_____

_____

_____

_____

_____

_____

_____

_____

_____

_____

_____

Then God said, "Let us make human beings in our image and likeness." (Genesis 1:26a ICB)

Do people sometimes say you look like your dad or your mom? The Bible says we are made to look like God, to reflect His image. We are not God, but people should be able to look at us and tell that we are His.

PARENT'S COMMENTS

_____

_____

_____

_____

_____

_____

_____

_____

_____

_____

_____

_____

Give us the food we need for
each day. (Matthew 6:11 ICB)

God does not give us everything we want,
but He does give us everything we need.
Thank Him for your lunch today.

PARENT'S COMMENTS

_____

_____

_____

_____

_____

_____

_____

_____

_____

_____

_____

Don't worry and say, "What will we eat?" or "What will we drink?" or "What will we wear?" All the people that don't know God keep trying to get these things. And your Father in heaven knows that you need them. (Matthew 6:31–32 ICB)

Do you get worried about things sometimes? God tells us not to worry, because He already knows what we need.

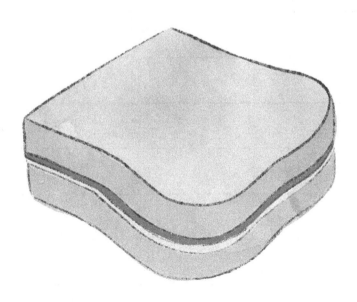

PARENT'S COMMENTS

_____

_____

_____

_____

_____

_____

_____

_____

_____

_____

_____

You are my friends if you do what
I command. (John 15:14 NLT)

Do you have some really great friends?
Jesus tells us that if we love Him and
obey Him, He will call us His friend. He
is the best friend you can ever have.

PARENT'S COMMENTS

_____

_____

_____

_____

_____

_____

_____

_____

_____

_____

_____

The Lord answered, "I myself will go with you. And I will give you rest." (Exodus 33:14 ICB)

Do you get really tired sometimes? Often worry makes us tired. Talk to God about whatever is making you tired or worried, and He will give you rest.

PARENT'S COMMENTS

_____

_____

_____

_____

_____

_____

_____

_____

_____

_____

_____

You will teach me God's way to live. Being with you will fill me with joy. At your right hand I will find pleasure forever. (Psalm 16:11 ICB)

We can be happy knowing that we are on the right path when we follow God.

PARENT'S COMMENTS

_____

_____

_____

_____

_____

_____

_____

_____

_____

_____

_____

_____

Yet I am always with you; you hold me
by my right hand. (Psalm 73:23 NIV)

Do you have a superhero? God is more
powerful than any superhero, and He
holds you by your right hand. You are safe.

PARENT'S COMMENTS

_____

_____

_____

_____

_____

_____

_____

_____

_____

_____

_____

_____

This God is our God forever
and ever. He will guide us from
now on. (Psalm 48:14 ICB)

*There is not one day of your life that God
is not walking beside you to guide you.*

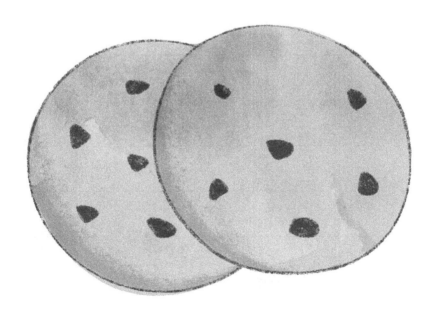

PARENT'S COMMENTS

_____

_____

_____

_____

_____

_____

_____

_____

_____

_____

_____

You have not seen Christ, but still you love him. You cannot see him now, but you believe in him. You are filled with a joy that cannot be explained. (1 Peter 1:8 ICB)

You can't see Jesus standing in front of you, but He is very real, and when you believe in Him, He will fill your heart with happiness.

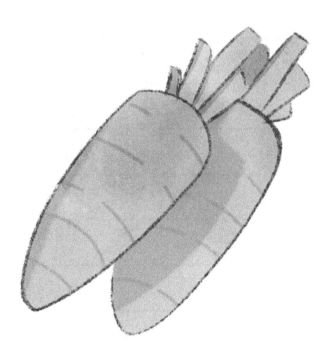

PARENT'S COMMENTS

_____

_____

_____

_____

_____

_____

_____

_____

_____

_____

_____

Don't think that you are better than you really are. (Romans 12:3b NLT)

If you are going to boast about anything, boast about the fact that Jesus loves you so much, He gave His life for you.

PARENT'S COMMENTS

_____

_____

_____

_____

_____

_____

_____

_____

_____

_____

_____

_____

The Word was full of grace and truth. From him we all received more and more blessings. (John 1:16 ICB)

All day long, Jesus blesses you. Look for those blessings, and give Him thanks.

PARENT'S COMMENTS

_____

_____

_____

_____

_____

_____

_____

_____

_____

_____

_____

Create in me a clean heart, O
God. Renew a loyal spirit within
me. (Psalm 51:10 NLT)

Some days we find ourselves upset
and thinking about the wrong things.
When that happens, we can ask God
to correct our thinking, and He will.

PARENT'S COMMENTS

_____

_____

_____

_____

_____

_____

_____

_____

_____

_____

_____

So we praise God for the
glorious grace he has poured
out on us who belong to his dear
Son. (Ephesians 1:6 NLT)

*A gift is free because someone gives it to us.
God sent Jesus so that we could know Him.
That is the best gift ever. Thank Him today.*

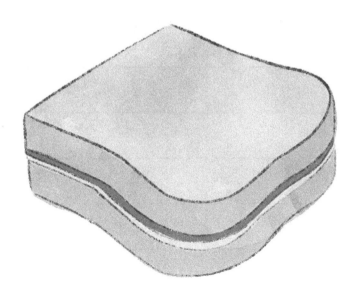

PARENT'S COMMENTS

_____

_____

_____

_____

_____

_____

_____

_____

_____

_____

_____

Walk in a manner worthy of
the Lord, fully pleasing to him.
(Colossians 1:10b ESV)

God has given you so much and loves
you so much. Just like you want to please
us, do the things that will please God.

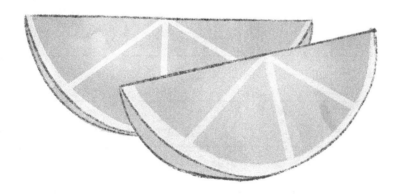

PARENT'S COMMENTS

_____

_____

_____

_____

_____

_____

_____

_____

_____

_____

_____

_____

He took me to a safe place.
Because he delights in me, he
saved me. (Psalm 18:19 ICB)

What brings you delight or happiness?
You bring God delight, and He will
always be there to help you.

PARENT'S COMMENTS

The eyes of the Lord are toward the righteous and his ears toward their cry. (Psalm 34:15 ESV)

God watches you all day long. If you need anything, just pray because He is always listening.

PARENT'S COMMENTS

_____

_____

_____

_____

_____

_____

_____

_____

_____

_____

_____

_____

_____

And this is the confidence that we have toward him, that if we ask anything according to his will, he hears us. (1 John 5:14 ESV)

It is important to ask God what He wants for you. He always wants what is best for you, so when you pray for that, He will gladly answer.

PARENT'S COMMENTS

_____

_____

_____

_____

_____

_____

_____

_____

_____

_____

_____

Then you will call on me and come
and pray to me, and I will hear
you. (Jeremiah 29:12 ESV)

Do you ever feel like no one is listening?
God promises to always listen. You can tell
Him what is on your mind at any time.

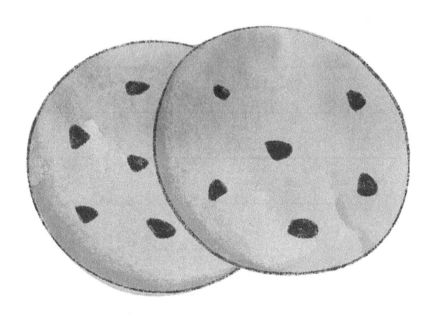

PARENT'S COMMENTS

_____

_____

_____

_____

_____

_____

_____

_____

_____

_____

_____

But, Lord, don't be far away.
You are my power. Hurry to
help me. (Psalm 22:19 ICB)

There will be some things that happen that
you just can't handle on your own. God
promises to help you and be your strength.

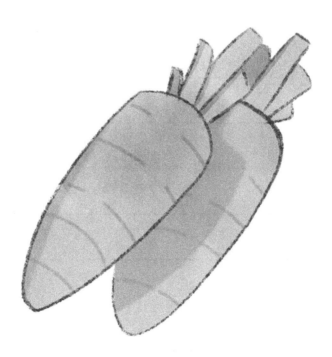

PARENT'S COMMENTS

_____

_____

_____

_____

_____

_____

_____

_____

_____

_____

_____

I praise you, because you made me in an amazing and wonderful way. (Psalm 139:14a ICB)

You are amazing, and God made you to be just who you are, unlike any other person. I thank God for you every day.

PARENT'S COMMENTS

_____

_____

_____

_____

_____

_____

_____

_____

_____

_____

_____

Oh Lord, God, you made the skies and the earth. You made them with your very great power. There is nothing too wonderful for you to do. (Jeremiah 32:17 ICB)

God made everything through His great power. There is not anything that He can't do.

PARENT'S COMMENTS

_____

_____

_____

_____

_____

_____

_____

_____

_____

_____

_____

And I am certain that God, who began the good work within you, will continue his work until it is finally finished on the day when Christ Jesus returns. (Philippians 1:6 NLT)

When you give your heart to Jesus, He promises to work every day on helping you become who He created you to be.

PARENT'S COMMENTS

_____

_____

_____

_____

_____

_____

_____

_____

_____

_____

_____

Most importantly, love each other deeply. Love has a way of not looking at others' sins. (1 Peter 4:8 ICB)

Even when someone is mean to you or hurts you, Jesus tells you to love them anyway. When you show them love, it helps them learn to act better.

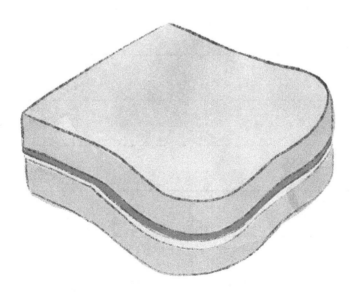

PARENT'S COMMENTS

_____

_____

_____

_____

_____

_____

_____

_____

_____

_____

_____

My command is this: Love each other
as I have loved you. (John 15:12 NIV)

Jesus loves you so very much, and
He wants you to love others.

PARENT'S COMMENTS

_____

_____

_____

_____

_____

_____

_____

_____

_____

_____

_____

I asked the Lord for help, and he answered me. He saved me from all that I feared. (Psalm 34:4 ICB)

If there is anything that you are fearful of or about today, talk to God about it. He wants to help you be fearless.

PARENT'S COMMENTS

_____

_____

_____

_____

_____

_____

_____

_____

_____

_____

_____

The Lord says, "Your thoughts are not like my thoughts. Your ways are not like my ways." (Isaiah 55:8 ICB)

Sometimes it is hard to understand why something happens. God knows everything, and He understands things that you and I don't. We just have to trust Him.

PARENT'S COMMENTS

_____

_____

_____

_____

_____

_____

_____

_____

_____

_____

_____

_____

God, my strength, I will sing praises to you. God, my protection, you are the God who loves me. (Psalm 59:17 ICB)

God says He will be your strength, and you can trust Him to protect you.

PARENT'S COMMENTS

_____

_____

_____

_____

_____

_____

_____

_____

_____

_____

_____

The Lord is my shepherd; I have all that I need. (Psalm 23:1 NLT)

A shepherd provides everything that the sheep need to survive. God has promised to do the same thing for you.

PARENT'S COMMENTS

_____

_____

_____

_____

_____

_____

_____

_____

_____

_____

_____

Every good action and every perfect gift is from God. (James 1:17a ICB)

Have you ever been given the perfect gift? It seemed so great at the time, but then it got old. The perfect gift that God gives you never gets old—it is His love.

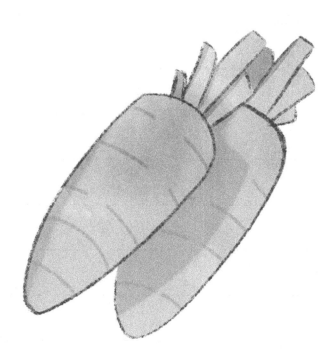

PARENT'S COMMENTS

The Lord your God goes with you. He will fight for you against your enemies. And he will save you. (Deuteronomy 20:4 ICB)

When you get mad at someone or someone picks on you, don't be mean back to them. Instead, let God handle it. He promises to defend you and give you victory.

PARENT'S COMMENTS

_____

_____

_____

_____

_____

_____

_____

_____

_____

_____

_____

_____

I told you these things so that you can have peace in me. In this world you will have trouble. But be brave! I have defeated the world (John 16:33 ICB)

When you are having trouble or feel upset, talk to God about it. He will make your heart feel much better.

PARENT'S COMMENTS

_____

_____

_____

_____

_____

_____

_____

_____

_____

_____

_____

_____

What, then, shall we say in response to these things? If God is for us, who can be against us? (Romans 8:31 NIV)

Have you ever felt like everyone was against you? The most important thing is to know that God, who is all powerful, is for you.

PARENT'S COMMENTS

_____

_____

_____

_____

_____

_____

_____

_____

_____

_____

_____

_____

But we thank God! He gives us the victory through our Lord Jesus Christ. (1 Corinthians 15:57 ICB)

Whenever you feel that you have done something amazing, remember that you are amazing, but it is God that made you that way and helps you. Thank Him first.

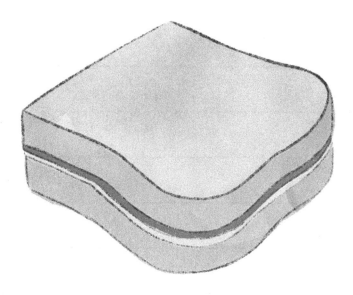

PARENT'S COMMENTS

_____

_____

_____

_____

_____

_____

_____

_____

_____

_____

_____

Let the peace that Christ gives control your thinking. (Colossians 3:15a ICB)

If you are feeling upset about something today, talk to God about it, and He will calm your heart and mind.

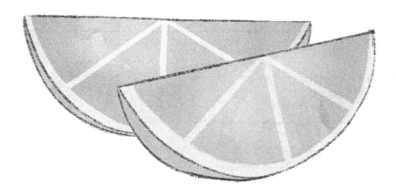

PARENT'S COMMENTS

_____

_____

_____

_____

_____

_____

_____

_____

_____

_____

_____

Give all your worries to him, because he cares for you. (1 Peter 5:7 ICB)

You can talk to God about anything. No matter how bad it is, He will help you work it out. No matter how confusing it is, He will help you understand it. He loves you very much!

PARENT'S COMMENTS

_____

_____

_____

_____

_____

_____

_____

_____

_____

_____

_____

The Lord gives strength to his people; the Lord blesses his people with peace. (Psalm 29:11 NIV)

If you feel like you can't do something, know that with God's help, you can. He will give you strength to do whatever you need to do.

PARENT'S COMMENTS

_____

_____

_____

_____

_____

_____

_____

_____

_____

_____

_____

Come to me, all of you who are tired and have heavy loads. I will give you rest. (Matthew 11:28 ICB)

God doesn't want you to be upset or worried. You can talk to Him about anything, and He will help you feel better, if you trust Him.

PARENT'S COMMENTS

_____

_____

_____

_____

_____

_____

_____

_____

_____

_____

_____

So we say with confidence, "The Lord is my helper; I will not be afraid." (Hebrews 13:6a NIV)

Whenever you are afraid, remember that God is your Helper and He will defend you.

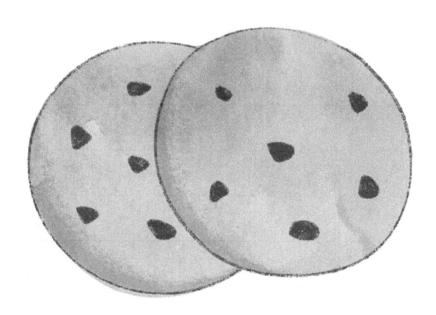

PARENT'S COMMENTS

_____

_____

_____

_____

_____

_____

_____

_____

_____

_____

_____

222

In Christ we can come before God with freedom and without fear. We can do this through faith in Christ. (Ephesians 3:12 ICB)

It may seem a little scary to talk to God because He is very powerful! However, because Jesus has called you His friend, you can talk to God at any time and not be afraid.

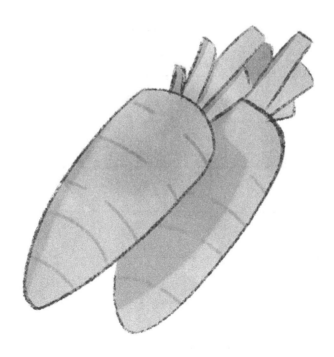

PARENT'S COMMENTS

_____

_____

_____

_____

_____

_____

_____

_____

_____

_____

_____

But they who wait for the Lord
shall renew their strength.
(Isaiah 40:31a ESV)

Sometimes it is very hard to wait for
something. God makes things happen
at just the right time. Ask Him, and
He will give you the patience to wait.

PARENT'S COMMENTS

_____

_____

_____

_____

_____

_____

_____

_____

_____

_____

_____

_____

The Lord is good to those whose hope is in him; to the one who seeks him, it is good to wait quietly for the salvation of the Lord. (Lamentations 3:25–26 NIV)

If you aren't sure about doing something, talk to God about it, and then wait for His answer. This is always the best thing to do.

PARENT'S COMMENTS

_____

_____

_____

_____

_____

_____

_____

_____

_____

_____

_____

_____

Wait for the Lord's help. Be strong and brave and wait for the Lord's help! (Psalm 27:14 ICB)

If someone is bothering you or bullying you, tell me about it. We will talk to God together and figure out the best thing to do.

PARENT'S COMMENTS

The Lord is great; He should be praised. (Psalm 48:1a ICB)

God is so great! Tell Him how great you think He is today.

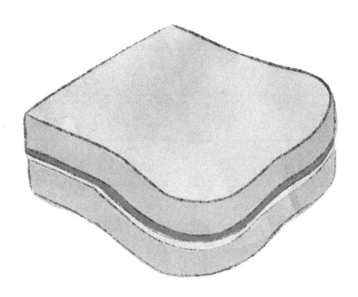

PARENT'S COMMENTS

_____

_____

_____

_____

_____

_____

_____

_____

_____

_____

_____

So our hope is in the Lord. He
is our help, our shield to protect
us. (Psalm 33:20 ICB)

Soldiers long ago used to carry a shield
to protect them from the arrows of their
enemies or from someone who tried to
attack them with a sword. God says that
He is your shield, and He will protect you.

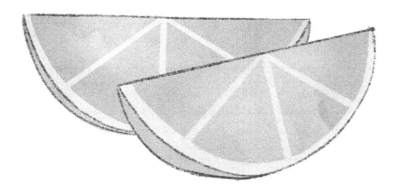

PARENT'S COMMENTS

_____

_____

_____

_____

_____

_____

_____

_____

_____

_____

_____

Let your unfailing love surround us, Lord, for our hope is in you alone. (Psalm 33:22 NLT)

God's love for you never changes. You can always trust Him and be excited about whatever He has planned for you.

PARENT'S COMMENTS

_____

_____

_____

_____

_____

_____

_____

_____

_____

_____

_____

For God loved the world so much that he gave his only Son. God gave his Son so that whoever believes in him may not be lost but have eternal life. (John 3:16 ICB)

God loves you so much that He gave you the thing that meant the most to Him. He gave His son for you so that you could be His child forever.

PARENT'S COMMENTS

_____

_____

_____

_____

_____

_____

_____

_____

_____

_____

_____

Later, Jesus talked to the people again. He said, "I am the light of the world. The person who follows me will never live in darkness. He will have the light that gives life." (John 8:12 ICB)

Have you ever walked into a dark room, and you were not sure which way to walk? Jesus said that He is the light that will shine into our dark places and show us the way to go.

PARENT'S COMMENTS

_____

_____

_____

_____

_____

_____

_____

_____

_____

_____

_____

_____

Understand this, my dear brothers and sisters: You must all be quick to listen, slow to speak, and slow to get angry. (James 1:19 NLT)

When you are angry, it is easy to want to say something mean or hurtful. Instead, take time to think about the right thing to say before you speak. Then try to work it out.

PARENT'S COMMENTS

_____

_____

_____

_____

_____

_____

_____

_____

_____

_____

_____

Those who work to bring peace are happy. God will call them his sons. (Matthew 5:9 ICB)

A peacemaker is someone who tries to understand others and help others understand each other and get along. God wants you to be a peacemaker.

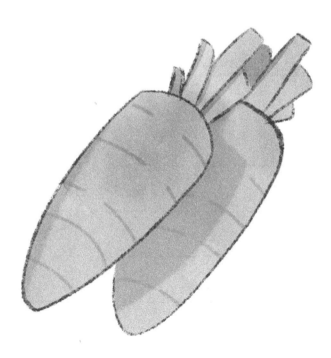

PARENT'S COMMENTS

_____

_____

_____

_____

_____

_____

_____

_____

_____

_____

_____

Do all that you can to live in peace
with everyone. (Romans 12:18 NLT)

Why is it so hard to get along with others?
Usually it is because we want our own way.
God wants us to think about what others
might want and try to work things out.

PARENT'S COMMENTS

_____

_____

_____

_____

_____

_____

_____

_____

_____

_____

_____

The Lord hears his people
when they call to Him for help.
He rescues them from all their
troubles. (Psalm 34:17 NLT)

*If you ever get fearful about something,
or you feel unable to get yourself
out of a situation, you can call out
to God, and He will help you.*

PARENT'S COMMENTS

_____

_____

_____

_____

_____

_____

_____

_____

_____

_____

_____

_____

Trust in the Lord with all your heart; do not depend on your own understanding. (Proverbs 3:5 NLT)

Sometimes things happen that you just don't understand. Since God knows everything, you can talk to Him about it and trust Him to help you better understand.

PARENT'S COMMENTS

_____

_____

_____

_____

_____

_____

_____

_____

_____

_____

_____

_____

He won't be afraid of bad news.
He is safe because he trusts
the Lord. (Psalm 112:7 ICB)

God tells you not to be afraid of
bad news. He already knows what
is going to happen, and He already
has a plan to work it all out.

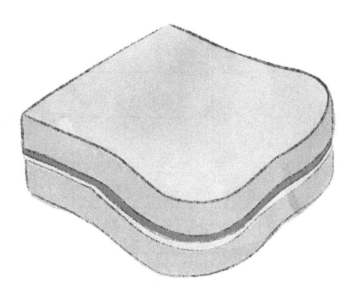

PARENT'S COMMENTS

_____

_____

_____

_____

_____

_____

_____

_____

_____

_____

_____

And yet, O Lord, you are our Father. We are the clay, and you are the potter. We all are formed by your hand. (Isaiah 64:8 NLT)

A potter is someone who takes an ugly peace of mud or clay and makes it into something beautiful. God is working to make you into someone very beautiful.

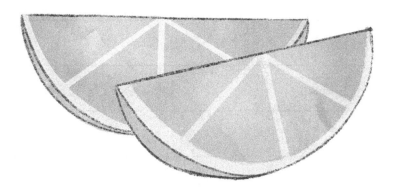

PARENT'S COMMENTS

_____

_____

_____

_____

_____

_____

_____

_____

_____

_____

_____

_____

Listen to advice and accept correction. Then in the end you will be wise. (Proverbs 19:20 ICB)

It is very important that you listen to your teacher and learn all that you can today. Be sure to ask questions if you don't understand something.

PARENT'S COMMENTS

Always work enthusiastically for the Lord, for you know that nothing you do for the Lord is ever useless. (1 Corinthians 15:58b NLT)

Sometimes you work hard, and it doesn't seem to make a difference. God says that He sees everything you do and encourages you to keep working hard.

PARENT'S COMMENTS

_____

_____

_____

_____

_____

_____

_____

_____

_____

_____

_____

_____

God is our protection and our
strength. He always helps in times
of trouble. (Psalm 46:1 ICB)

If you are having trouble today, remember
that God is always there to help you.

PARENT'S COMMENTS

_____

_____

_____

_____

_____

_____

_____

_____

_____

_____

_____

The Lord defends those who
suffer. He protects them in times
of trouble. (Psalm 9:9 ICB)

*If you feel like everything is going wrong
for you today, remember God is in
control, and He is working it all out.*

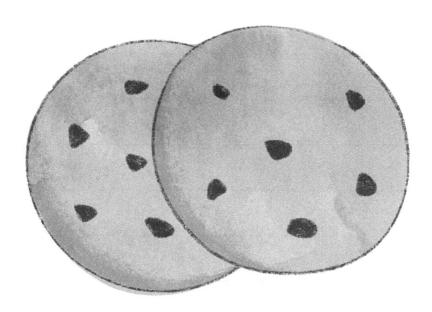

PARENT'S COMMENTS

_____

_____

_____

_____

_____

_____

_____

_____

_____

_____

_____

The Father has loved us so much! He loved us so much that we are called children of God. And we really are his children! (1 John 3:1a ICB)

You are God's child, and He loves you very much. He only wants what is good for you, and He has promised to give you good things.

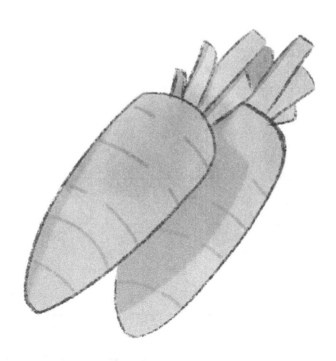

PARENT'S COMMENTS

_____

_____

_____

_____

_____

_____

_____

_____

_____

_____

_____

But you may suffer for doing right. Even if that happens, you are blessed. (1 Peter 3:14a ICB)

If you do something good and someone makes fun of you, don't worry. God says He will bless you.

PARENT'S COMMENTS

His God instructs him and teaches him the right way. (Isaiah 28:26 NIV)

When you listen to God, you know that you are being taught the right thing.

PARENT'S COMMENTS

_____

_____

_____

_____

_____

_____

_____

_____

_____

_____

_____

The Lord gives me strength and makes me sing. He has saved me. (Exodus 15:2a ICB)

God will make you strong, and He will always save you.

PARENT'S COMMENTS

For I, the Lord your God, hold your right hand; it is I who say to you, "Fear not, I am the one who helps you." (Isaiah 41:13 ESV)

Do you feel safer in a scary situation when someone stronger holds your hand? God promises to always hold your hand through hard things.

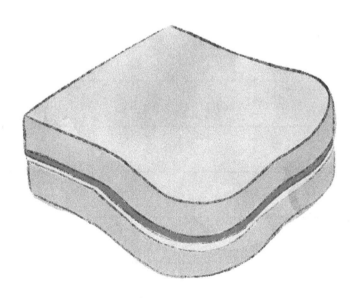

PARENT'S COMMENTS

_____

_____

_____

_____

_____

_____

_____

_____

_____

_____

_____

Depend on the Lord in whatever you do. Then your plans will succeed. (Proverbs 16:3 ICB)

Check with God before you do something, and He will help it turn out good.

PARENT'S COMMENTS

_____

_____

_____

_____

_____

_____

_____

_____

_____

_____

_____

_____

And my God will supply every need of yours according to his riches in glory in Christ Jesus. (Philippians 4:19 ESV)

God has promised to supply everything you need for today.

PARENT'S COMMENTS

_____

_____

_____

_____

_____

_____

_____

_____

_____

_____

_____

_____

Give your worries to the Lord. He will take care of you. He will never let good people down. (Psalm 55:22 ICB)

If something is bothering you today, turn it over to God. He wants to help you with everything. He will help you do the right thing.

PARENT'S COMMENTS

_____

_____

_____

_____

_____

_____

_____

_____

_____

_____

_____

But the Lord said to me, "My grace is enough for you. When you are weak, then my power is made perfect in you." (2 Corinthians 12:9a ICB)

If you feel that you can't do something, God can. He wants you to understand that you need His help in everything.

PARENT'S COMMENTS

_____

_____

_____

_____

_____

_____

_____

_____

_____

_____

_____

_____

The heavens tell the glory of God. And the skies announce what his hands have made. (Psalm 19:1 ICB)

God created everything around you. Just look around outside and see how amazing He is!

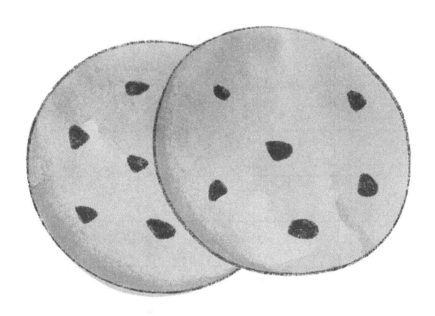

PARENT'S COMMENTS

_____

_____

_____

_____

_____

_____

_____

_____

_____

_____

_____

Jesus said to him, "I am the way, and the truth, and the life. No one comes to the Father except through me." (John 14:6 ESV)

The only way to heaven is Jesus. Don't believe anything else that you hear. Jesus came to give you life.

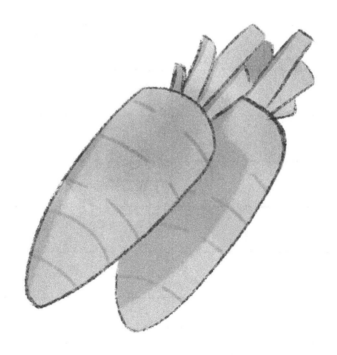

PARENT'S COMMENTS

Come now, let us reason together,
says the Lord… (Isaiah 1:18a ESV)

To reason together means to talk about
things together. God wants you to talk to
Him and listen to Him about everything.

PARENT'S COMMENTS

_____

_____

_____

_____

_____

_____

_____

_____

_____

_____

_____

_____

You will have many kinds of troubles. But when these things happen, you should be happy. (James 1:2 ICB)

When you have a bad day, God wants you to choose to be happy anyway because He is working it all out for good.

PARENT'S COMMENTS

_____

_____

_____

_____

_____

_____

_____

_____

_____

_____

_____

The Lord says, "I will make you wise. I will show you where to go. I will guide you and watch over you." (Psalm 32:8 ICB)

If you were lost in the woods, you would need a guide to show you the way. God wants to be your guide each day. He sees everything and knows the way you should go.

PARENT'S COMMENTS

_____

_____

_____

_____

_____

_____

_____

_____

_____

_____

_____

If you go the wrong way—to the right or to the left—you will hear a voice behind you. It will say, "You should go this way. This is the right way." (Isaiah 30:21 ICB)

Sometimes you get distracted and go the wrong way. God is always walking with you and wants to help get you back on the right path.

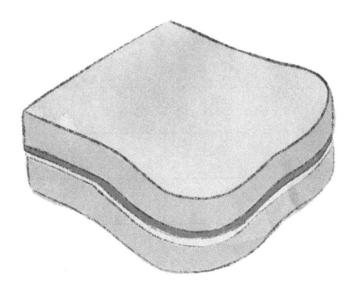

PARENT'S COMMENTS

_____

_____

_____

_____

_____

_____

_____

_____

_____

_____

_____

Finally, be strong in the Lord
and in the strength of his might.
(Ephesians 6:10 ESV)

God is the most powerful of
anyone. He is always there to help
you be strong and successful.

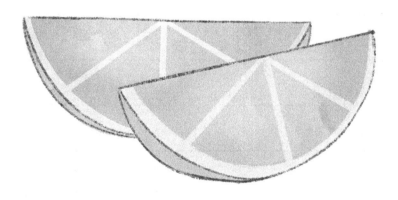

PARENT'S COMMENTS

_____

_____

_____

_____

_____

_____

_____

_____

_____

_____

_____

_____

Call to Me and I will answer you, and will tell you great and hidden things that you have not known. (Jeremiah 33:3 ESV)

If you talk to God each day, He will teach and show you amazing things that you did not know.

PARENT'S COMMENTS

_____

_____

_____

_____

_____

_____

_____

_____

_____

_____

_____

Without faith no one can please
God. Anyone who comes to God
must believe that he is real and that
he rewards those who truly want
to find him. (Hebrews 11:6 ICB)

*If you want to please God, have faith in
Him to always give you what you need.*

PARENT'S COMMENTS

_____

_____

_____

_____

_____

_____

_____

_____

_____

_____

_____

_____

Enter by the narrow gate. For the gate is wide and the way is easy that leads to destruction, and those who enter it are many. (Matthew 7:13 ESV)

The right thing to do is not always the easy thing to do. However, doing the right thing is always the best thing to do.

PARENT'S COMMENTS

_____

_____

_____

_____

_____

_____

_____

_____

_____

_____

_____

Those who know the Lord trust him. He will not leave those who come to him. (Psalm 9:10 ICB)

The more you get to know God, the more you know you can trust Him. He will never leave you alone.

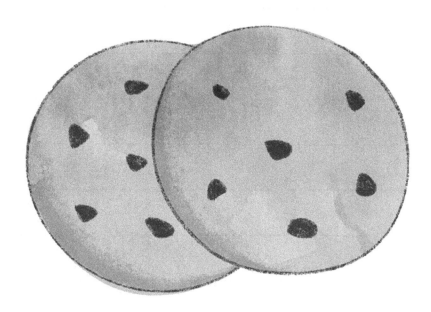

PARENT'S COMMENTS

_____

_____

_____

_____

_____

_____

_____

_____

_____

_____

_____

_____

Being afraid of people can get you into trouble. But if you trust the Lord, you will be safe. (Proverbs 29:25 ICB)

People can sometimes be scary. Tell an adult if you are scared, then trust God to keep you safe.

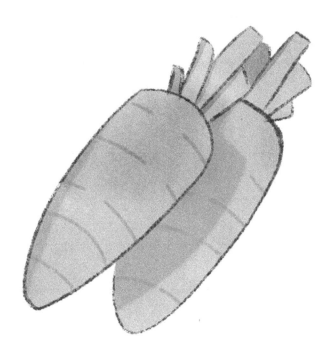

PARENT'S COMMENTS

You were running a good race. You were obeying the truth. Who stopped you from following the true way? (Galatians 5:7 ICB

You are a good person. Don't let anyone talk you into doing something you know is wrong.

PARENT'S COMMENTS

_____

_____

_____

_____

_____

_____

_____

_____

_____

_____

_____

_____

I have fought the good fight, I have finished the race, I have kept the faith. (2 Timothy 4:7 ESV)

When you are in a race, you want to win. Do what you know is right every day, and you will win your race to follow Jesus.

PARENT'S COMMENTS

_____

_____

_____

_____

_____

_____

_____

_____

_____

_____

_____

_____

Even lions may become weak and hungry. But those people who go to the Lord for help will have every good thing. (Psalm 34:10 ICB)

God has so many good things that He wants to give you and do for you. Follow Him every day.

PARENT'S COMMENTS

_____

_____

_____

_____

_____

_____

_____

_____

_____

_____

_____

_____

Our Lord is great and very powerful. There is no limit to what he knows. (Psalm 147:5 ICB)

God is very powerful and great. He understands everything about you because He created you.

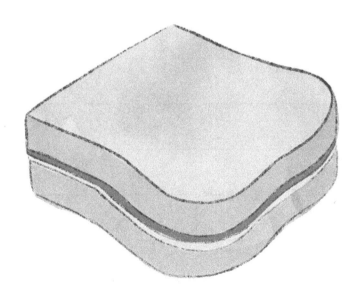

PARENT'S COMMENTS

_____

_____

_____

_____

_____

_____

_____

_____

_____

_____

_____

Be joyful because you have hope.
Be patient when trouble comes. Pray
at all times. (Romans 12:12 ICB)

Being happy and patient is
sometimes hard, especially when
things aren't going good. Pray that
God will help you and He will.

PARENT'S COMMENTS

_____

_____

_____

_____

_____

_____

_____

_____

_____

_____

_____

In all the work you are doing, work the best you can. Work as if you were working for the Lord, not for men. (Colossians 3:23 ICB)

If Jesus were your teacher, would you be on your best behavior and work hard? Well, work today just like you would work for Him.

PARENT'S COMMENTS

_____

_____

_____

_____

_____

_____

_____

_____

_____

_____

_____

Lord, every morning you hear my voice. Every morning, I tell you what I need. And I wait for your answer. (Psalm 5:3 ICB)

Pray every morning before you start your day. Then watch and see what God will do.

PARENT'S COMMENTS

_____

_____

_____

_____

_____

_____

_____

_____

_____

_____

_____

Do you think I am trying to make people accept me? No! God is the one I am trying to please. (Galatians 1:10a ICB)

The most important person you can try to please today is Jesus.

PARENT'S COMMENTS

_____

_____

_____

_____

_____

_____

_____

_____

_____

_____

_____

When you talk, do not say harmful things. But say what people need— words that will help others become stronger. (Ephesians 4:29a ICB)

Think about what you say to others today. Say only things that will make them feel good about themselves and encourage them.

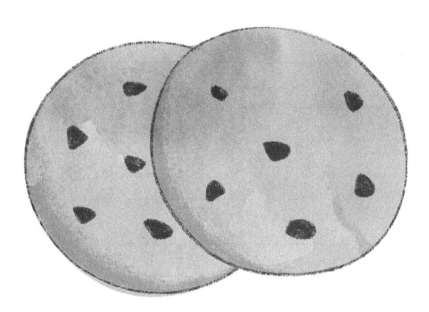

PARENT'S COMMENTS

_____

_____

_____

_____

_____

_____

_____

_____

_____

_____

_____

_____

Whoever restrains his words has knowledge, and he who has a cool spirit is a man of understanding. (Proverbs 17:27 ESV)

To restrain your words means to be careful what you say. If you are angry, be quiet until you are no longer angry. Then talk it out.

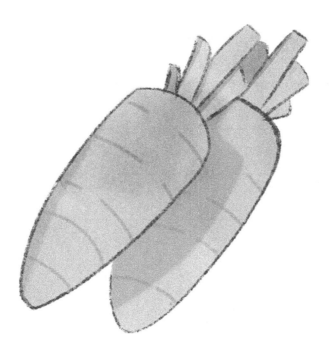

PARENT'S COMMENTS

_____

_____

_____

_____

_____

_____

_____

_____

_____

_____

_____

I rejoice in your word like one
who discovers a great treasure.
(Psalm 119:162 NLT)

Reading God's Word is like finding a
great treasure. It should always make you
happy to read or listen to God's Word.

PARENT'S COMMENTS

Your Word is a lamp to guide
my feet and a light for my path.
(Psalm 119:105 NLT)

God's Word, your Bible, helps you
know the right thing to do and say.
It is the *best* book because every
word was inspired by God.

PARENT'S COMMENTS

_____

_____

_____

_____

_____

_____

_____

_____

_____

_____

_____

Set a guard, O Lord, over my
mouth; keep watch over the door
of my lips! (Psalm 141:3 ESV)

To guard something means to protect
it. God wants to protect you by helping
you say the right thing today.

PARENT'S COMMENTS

_____

_____

_____

_____

_____

_____

_____

_____

_____

_____

_____

Those who want to do right more than anything else are happy. God will fully satisfy them. (Matthew 5:6 ICB)

Remember when you feel really hungry? All you want to do is find something to eat. God wants you to feel that way about obeying Him. He wants that to be very important to you.

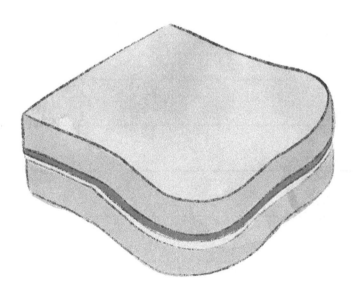

PARENT'S COMMENTS

_____

_____

_____

_____

_____

_____

_____

_____

_____

_____

Praise the Lord; praise God our savior! For each day he carried us in his arms. (Psalm 68:19 NLT)

If you are carrying something really heavy, it is nice when someone carries it for you. God wants to help carry all the things that are hard for you.

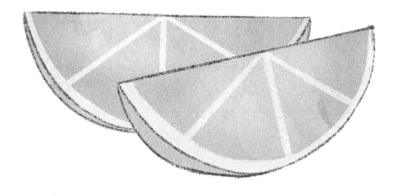

PARENT'S COMMENTS

_____

_____

_____

_____

_____

_____

_____

_____

_____

_____

_____

God looked down from heaven at all the people. He looked to see if anyone was wise, if anyone was looking to God for help. (Psalm 53:2 ICB)

God is always watching over us, and He wants us to always ask Him for help.

PARENT'S COMMENTS

_____

_____

_____

_____

_____

_____

_____

_____

_____

_____

_____

_____

The one who calls you is faithful, and he will do it. (1 Thessalonians 5:24 NIV)

God always keeps His promises. You can always count on Him to love you and take care of you.

PARENT'S COMMENTS

_____

_____

_____

_____

_____

_____

_____

_____

_____

_____

_____

You should be a light for other people. Live so that they will see the good things you do. Live so that they will praise your Father in heaven. (Matthew 5:16 ICB)

When you do good things, people will see and want to know more about God.

PARENT'S COMMENTS

_____

_____

_____

_____

_____

_____

_____

_____

_____

_____

_____

Each of you should use whatever
gift you have received to serve
others. (1 Peter 4:10a NIV)

*You are very good at being kind to others.
Find people that you can help today.*

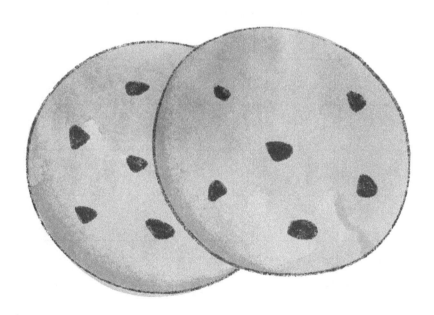

PARENT'S COMMENTS

_____

_____

_____

_____

_____

_____

_____

_____

_____

_____

_____

_____

For we are God's handiwork, created in Christ Jesus to do good works, which God prepared in advance for us to do. (Ephesians 2:10 NIV)

God has some very special things planned for you to do that only you can do. Always ask Him what He wants you to do, then do it.

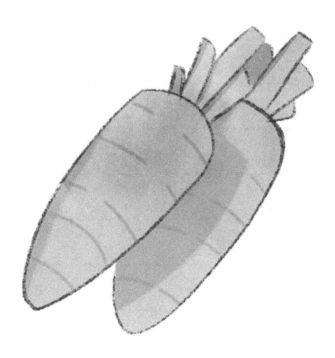

PARENT'S COMMENTS

_____

_____

_____

_____

_____

_____

_____

_____

_____

_____

_____

_____

Do not be interested only in your own life, but be interested in the lives of others. (Philippians 2:4 ICB)

Find ways that you can help others today.

PARENT'S COMMENTS

You, Lord, give true peace. You give peace to those who depend on you. You give peace to those who trust you. So trust the Lord always. (Isaiah 26:3–4a ICB)

You know that God loves you very much. Trust Him today.

PARENT'S COMMENTS

_____

_____

_____

_____

_____

_____

_____

_____

_____

_____

_____

_____

You can be sure that I will be with you always. I will continue with you until the end of the world. (Matthew 28:20b ICB)

Be aware that God is with you every day and every night. He never leaves you.

PARENT'S COMMENTS

_____

_____

_____

_____

_____

_____

_____

_____

_____

_____

_____

It is better to be poor and respect the Lord than to be wealthy and have much trouble. (Proverbs 15:16 ICB)

It doesn't matter if you have a lot of things. What matters is if you love and follow God.

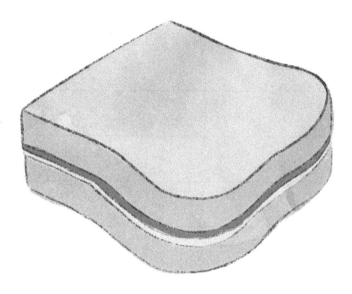

PARENT'S COMMENTS

_____

_____

_____

_____

_____

_____

_____

_____

_____

_____

_____

_____

Do not think that you are better than you are. (Romans 12:3b ICB)

You are such a great person, but instead of thinking that about yourself, show that by the way you act toward others. Know that God helps you, and give Him the credit for all things.

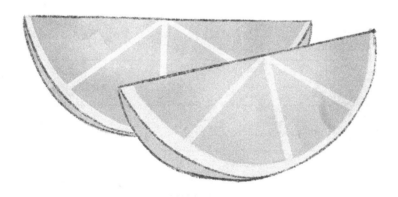

PARENT'S COMMENTS

_____

_____

_____

_____

_____

_____

_____

_____

_____

_____

_____

The Light shines in the darkness. And the darkness has not overpowered the Light. (John 1:5 ICB)

Have you ever been in a dark room and turned on a flashlight? The light helps you find your way in the darkness. That's what Jesus does. He helps us find our way every day.

PARENT'S COMMENTS

_____

_____

_____

_____

_____

_____

_____

_____

_____

_____

_____

No man has ever seen God. But God the only Son is very close to the Father. And the Son has shown us what God is like. (John 1:18 ICB)

If you want to know what God is like, learn more about Jesus. He and the Father are One.

PARENT'S COMMENTS

_____

_____

_____

_____

_____

_____

_____

_____

_____

_____

_____

_____

Let me hear of your unfailing love
each morning, for I am trusting
you. (Psalm 143:8a NLT)

Every morning, remember how much
God loves you, and trust Him each day.

PARENT'S COMMENTS

_____

_____

_____

_____

_____

_____

_____

_____

_____

_____

_____

I will look to the Lord for help. I will wait for God to save me. My God will hear me. (Micah 7:7 ICB)

Sometimes we have to wait for God to answer our prayers, but He always hears us.

PARENT'S COMMENTS

_____

_____

_____

_____

_____

_____

_____

_____

_____

_____

_____

So we praise God for the glorious grace he has poured out on us who belong to his dear Son. (Ephesians 1:6 NLT)

You don't have to do anything to become a child of God except believe in Jesus and trust Him.

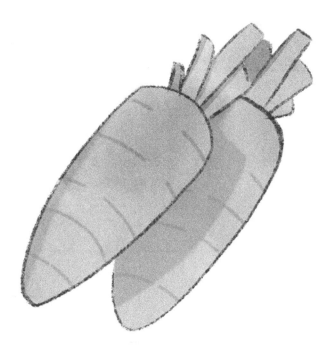

PARENT'S COMMENTS

_____

_____

_____

_____

_____

_____

_____

_____

_____

_____

_____

You have been saved by grace because you believe. You did not save yourselves. It was a gift from God. (Ephesians 2:8 ICB)

Jesus is your friend, not because you do good things, but because He is good and He loves you.

PARENT'S COMMENTS

_____

_____

_____

_____

_____

_____

_____

_____

_____

_____

_____

_____

Give all your worries to him, because
he cares for you. (1 Peter 5:7 ICB)

Jesus loves you so much, and He cares
about everything that happens in your
life. Talk to Him about everything.

PARENT'S COMMENTS

_____

_____

_____

_____

_____

_____

_____

_____

_____

_____

_____

Trust in the Lord forever, for the Lord, the Lord himself, is the Rock eternal. (Isaiah 26:4 NIV)

Trust God every day. He is strong like a rock, and He is always there for you.

PARENT'S COMMENTS

_____

_____

_____

_____

_____

_____

_____

_____

_____

_____

_____

_____

You will only need to remain
calm. The Lord will fight for
you. (Exodus 14:14 ICB)

If you get mad at someone, just smile,
walk away, and let God handle it.

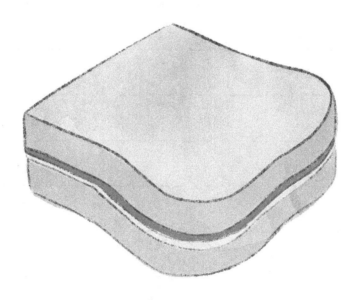

PARENT'S COMMENTS

_____

_____

_____

_____

_____

_____

_____

_____

_____

_____

_____

_____

_____

For I, the Lord your God, hold your right hand; it is I who say to you, "Fear not, I am the one who helps you." (Isaiah 41:13 ESV)

Whenever you get afraid, just imagine that God is holding your hand and will take care of you. He promises to do that.

PARENT'S COMMENTS

_____

_____

_____

_____

_____

_____

_____

_____

_____

_____

_____

_____

You have kept count of my tossings; put my tears in your bottle. Are they not in your book? (Psalm 56:8 ESV)

God loves you so much that when you cry, He is sad, and He says that He saves all of your tears in a bottle.

PARENT'S COMMENTS

_____

_____

_____

_____

_____

_____

_____

_____

_____

_____

_____

_____

Yes, God even knows how many hairs you have on your head. Don't be afraid. You are worth much more than many sparrows. (Luke 12:7 ICB)

God takes care of the birds, and you are so much more valuable to Him than they are. He even knows the number of hairs on your head. Isn't that amazing?

PARENT'S COMMENTS

_____

_____

_____

_____

_____

_____

_____

_____

_____

_____

_____

Behold, I have engraved you
on the palms of my hands; your
walls are continually before
me. (Isaiah 49:16 ESV)

Have you ever written something on
your hand that you want to remember?
God has permanently put your name
on His hand. He never forgets you.

PARENT'S COMMENTS

_____

_____

_____

_____

_____

_____

_____

_____

_____

_____

_____

The Lord your God is with you. The mighty One will save you. The Lord will be happy with you. You will rest in his love. He will sing and be joyful about you. (Zephaniah 3:17 ICB)

You make God very happy. When you are upset, He will quiet you with His love and help you. He sings songs about you.

PARENT'S COMMENTS

_____

_____

_____

_____

_____

_____

_____

_____

_____

_____

_____

_____

In the same way, there is joy before the angels of God when one sinner changes his heart. (Luke 15:10 ICB)

When you ask Jesus to forgive you and save you, the angels throw a party in heaven.

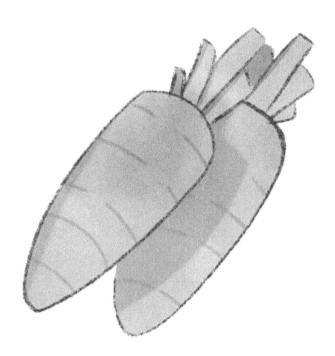

PARENT'S COMMENTS

_____

_____

_____

_____

_____

_____

_____

_____

_____

_____

_____

With God's power working in us,
God can do much, much more
than anything we can ask or
think of. (Ephesians 3:20 ICB)

God is able to do more for you
than you could ever imagine.

PARENT'S COMMENTS

_____

_____

_____

_____

_____

_____

_____

_____

_____

_____

_____

I go to bed and sleep in peace. Lord, only you keep me safe. (Psalm 4:8 ICB)

God is the one Who can keep you safe, every day and every night, so you don't ever have to be afraid.

PARENT'S COMMENTS

_____

_____

_____

_____

_____

_____

_____

_____

_____

_____

_____

_____

For thus says the Lord God, "Behold I, I, myself will search for my sheep and seek them out." (Ezekiel 34:11 ESV)

Just like a shepherd searches for his sheep that wander away, God always does what it takes to bring you back close to him.

PARENT'S COMMENTS

_____

_____

_____

_____

_____

_____

_____

_____

_____

_____

_____

_____

Search for the Lord and for
his strength; continually seek
him. (Psalm 105:4 NLT)

When you are feeling weak, always turn
to God. He will be your strength.

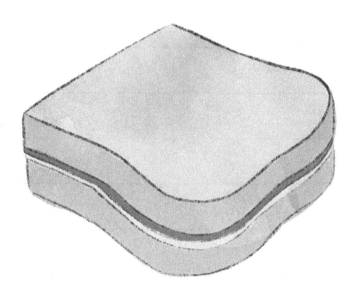

PARENT'S COMMENTS

_____

_____

_____

_____

_____

_____

_____

_____

_____

_____

_____

_____

A gentle answer will calm a person's anger. But an unkind answer will cause more anger. (Proverbs 15:1 ICB)

Always answer someone with kindness. This keeps many arguments from happening.

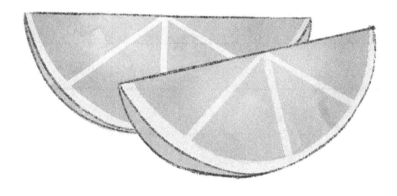

PARENT'S COMMENTS

_____

_____

_____

_____

_____

_____

_____

_____

_____

_____

_____

God will continue to be true
even when every person is
false. (Romans 3:4a ICB)

*Even when you feel like you can't count
on anyone else, you can count on God.*

PARENT'S COMMENTS

_____

_____

_____

_____

_____

_____

_____

_____

_____

_____

That I may declare your praises
in the gates of Daughter Zion,
and there rejoice in your
salvation. (Psalm 9:14 NIV)

To praise God means to know how great
He is and to tell others. It is always
good to tell people how great God is.

PARENT'S COMMENTS

_____

_____

_____

_____

_____

_____

_____

_____

_____

_____

But I trust in your unfailing love.
I will rejoice because you have
rescued me. (Psalm 13:5 NLT)

*Be happy today that you can completely
trust God and His love for you.*

PARENT'S COMMENTS

_____

_____

_____

_____

_____

_____

_____

_____

_____

_____

_____

Do not forget to do good to others. And share with them what you have. These are the sacrifices that please God. (Hebrews 13:16 ICB)

When you do good things for others and share with them, this pleases God.

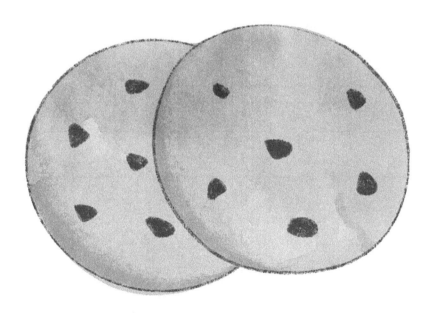

PARENT'S COMMENTS

_____

_____

_____

_____

_____

_____

_____

_____

_____

_____

_____

But God showed his great love for us by sending Christ to die for us while we were still sinners. (Romans 5:8 NLT)

God doesn't wait until we are good enough to show us how much He loves us. His love is sure every day.

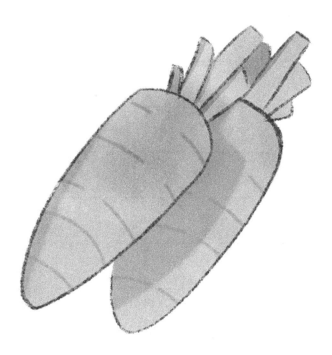

PARENT'S COMMENTS

_____

_____

_____

_____

_____

_____

_____

_____

_____

_____

_____

You cannot add any time to your life by worrying about it. (Matthew 6:27 ICB)

Worry never makes life better. Trust that God has your whole life planned out, and His is a great plan.

PARENT'S COMMENTS

_____

_____

_____

_____

_____

_____

_____

_____

_____

_____

_____

_____

ABOUT THE AUTHOR

Myrna Conrad is a Christian author of fiction and inspirational writings. She has published one fiction book, *Discarded Lives*, and has been published in *The Upper Room* and GO magazine. Myrna currently writes a monthly column in *Destin Life* and *Bay Life* local newspapers.

Myrna started writing a daily devotional thought to share with her son in his lunchbox when he was in high school. At the end of his senior year, many of his friends and teachers shared how these daily notes had impacted them as well. She didn't think to do this with her daughter who is three years older. However, years later, when everyone had cell phones, she started texting an inspirational scripture and thought to all of her family members. This soon grew to include friends and others who requested this daily text. This led to the idea of writing her children's devotional book, *Lunchbox Devotions for Kids*.

Myrna currently lives in Destin, Florida, with her husband, Bob. She enjoys spending time and sharing adventures with her husband, her two children, their spouses, and her four grandchildren. You can visit her website at www.myrnaconrad.com

Printed in the USA
CPSIA information can be obtained
at www.ICGtesting.com
LVHW091436291023
762483LV00042B/350